KT-472-900

Recipes and Photography by
Sandra Mahut

MUG CAKES
★*chocolate*★

Ready in 2 minutes in the microwave!

Illustrations by Jane Teasdale

hardie grant books

contents

....

making mug cakes

mug cake

A mug cake takes approximately 2 minutes to cook in the microwave. For chocolate mug cakes, the method is almost always the same: begin by melting the butter and chocolate in the mug, whisk, add the other ingredients and briskly whisk once more. Put in the microwave to cook. It rises in 2 minutes and then it's ready to eat!

quantities

A mug cake is a real homemade cake using all the ingredients you would put in a regualr cake. However, it takes a fraction of the time and is cooked in a mug in the microwave! The only equipment you require is a mug, a fork or whisk and (sometimes) a bowl. There's no need to weigh anything – all the quantities are given in spoonfuls.

equivalent weights

Here are the equivalent weights for the measures used in the recipes:

1 tablespoon flour/sugar **= 15 g (½ oz)**
1 teaspoon flour/sugar **– 5 g (0.2 oz)**
½ teaspoon baking powder **= 2 g (0.1 oz)**
1 slice butter **1 cm (½ in) thick = 30 g (1 oz)**
1 slice butter **½ cm (¼ in) thick = 15 g (½ oz)**
1 square of chocolate **= 5 g (0.2 oz)**

chocolate

Chocolate can be tricky to cook. It is important not to overheat the mixture or it can burn.

Be experimental with your mug cake and try out different chocolate combinations – they will all be delicious! Alternatively you can opt for the chocolate flavour you like best and customise it however you like.

mugs & microwaves

A standard **mug** holds **300 ml (10 fl oz)**. **Set** the microwave power to **800 watts**.

a few tips

Making mug cakes is a delicate process. Microwave cooking can be unpredictable so you may have to try it a few times to get the best result. To get a smooth, even mixture, use a fork or a mini whisk. The batter has to be mixed vigorously in the mug to make sure the cake cooks evenly.

Sometimes a mug cake can rise too high or overflow: either the mixture contains too much butter, or the mug is too small or narrow. It's simply a matter of trial and error, so if your first attempt doesn't work, just try it again!

One fail-safe trick for getting a melting middle is to cook the mug cake for 45 seconds in the microwave, then remove the mug and push the melting ingredient into the centre of the mixture. Return the mug to the microwave and cook for a further 45 seconds.

Another tip for a lighter, fluffier mug cake is to use almond butter instead of regular butter.

Decorate your mug cake in your own way – with icing (confectioners') sugar or whipped cream, a glaze of icing (frosting) with citrus zest, food colouring or chocolate sprinkles...

classic cocoa
mug cake

....

INGREDIENTS

1 slice of butter 1 cm (½ in) thick
   (30 g/1 oz)
1 egg
2 tablespoons caster (superfine) sugar
1 tablespoon vanilla sugar or
   1 teaspoon vanilla extract
2 tablespoons unsweetened
   cocoa powder
4 tablespoons plain (all-purpose) flour
½ teaspoon baking powder

DECORATION

½ teaspoon cocoa powder

In a mug: melt the butter in the microwave for 30 seconds (800 watts).

One by one, whisk in the egg, sugar, vanilla sugar, cocoa, flour and baking powder. Cook in the microwave for 1 minute 20 seconds (800 watts).

Dust with cocoa powder. Allow to cool for 1 minute before eating.

dark chocolate
fondant mug cake

....

INGREDIENTS

1 slice of butter 1 cm (½ in) thick
  (30 g/1 oz)
8 squares of dark chocolate (40 g/1½ oz)
  at least 55 % cocoa
1 egg
2 tablespoons caster (superfine) sugar
4 tablespoons plain (all-purpose) flour
½ teaspoon baking powder

In a mug: melt the butter with the chocolate in the microwave for 30–40 seconds (800 watts).

Beat the mixture until smooth, then allow it to cool slightly. One by one, whisk in the egg, sugar, flour and baking powder. Cook in the microwave for 1 minute 20 seconds (800 watts).

Allow to cool for 1 minute before eating.

classic milk chocolate
mug cake

....

INGREDIENTS

1 slice of butter 1 cm (½ in) thick
   (30 g/1 oz)
6 squares of milk chocolate (30 g/1 oz)
1 egg
2 tablespoons caster (superfine) sugar
1½ teaspoons vanilla sugar or
   ½ teaspoon vanilla extract
4½ tablespoons plain (all-purpose) flour
½ teaspoon baking powder

In a mug: melt the butter with the chocolate in the microwave for 30–40 seconds (800 watts).

Beat the mixture until smooth, then allow it to cool slightly. One by one, whisk in the egg, sugar, vanilla sugar, flour and baking powder. Cook in the microwave for 1 minute 20 seconds (800 watts).

Allow to cool for 1 minute before eating.

white chocolate
fondant mug cake

....

INGREDIENTS

1 slice of butter 1 cm (½ in) thick
    (30 g/1 oz)
6 squares of white chocolate (30 g/1 oz)
1 egg
2 tablespoons caster (superfine) sugar
4 tablespoons plain (all-purpose) flour
½ teaspoon baking powder

In a mug: melt the butter with the chocolate in the microwave for 40 seconds (800 watts).

Beat the mixture until smooth, then allow it to cool slightly. One by one, whisk in the egg, sugar, flour and baking powder. Cook in the microwave for 1 minute 30 seconds (800 watts).

Allow to cool for 1 minute before eating.

milk chocolate
crunchy mug cake

....

INGREDIENTS

1 slice of butter ½ cm (¼ in) thick
  (15 g/½ oz)
5 squares of milk chocolate with crisped
  rice (such as Crunch®, 40 g/1½ oz)
1 teaspoon unsweetened cocoa powder
1 egg
1 teaspoon single (light) cream
2 tablespoons caster (superfine) sugar
4 tablespoons plain (all-purpose) flour
½ teaspoon baking powder
1 tablespoon puffed rice (such as
  Rice Krispies®)

DECORATION

1 teaspoon puffed rice (such as
  Rice Krispies®)

In a mug: melt the butter with the chocolate in the microwave for 40 seconds (800 watts).

Beat the mixture until smooth, then allow it to cool slightly. One by one, whisk in the cocoa powder, egg, cream, sugar, flour and baking powder. Add the puffed rice without stirring too much. Cook in the microwave for 1 minute 30 seconds (800 watts) then decorate with puffed rice.

Allow to cool for 1 minute before eating.

big mug cake
for sharing

....

INGREDIENTS

1 slice of butter 2 cm (¾ in) thick
  (60 g/2 oz) or 60 g (2 oz) almond butter
12 squares of dark or milk chocolate
  (60 g/2 oz)
2 eggs
4 tablespoons light brown sugar
1 tablespoon vanilla sugar or
  1 teaspoon vanilla extract
1 drop of almond extract
8 tablespoons plain (all-purpose) flour
2 tablespoons ground almonds
1 level teaspoon baking powder

DECORATION

a few flaked (slivered) almonds

In a big mug: melt the butter with the chocolate in the microwave for 50 seconds (800 watts).

Beat the mixture until smooth, then allow it to cool slightly. One by one, whisk in the eggs, sugar, vanilla sugar, almond extract, flour, ground almonds and baking powder. Cook in the microwave for 2 minutes 30 seconds (800 watts).

Allow to cool for 1 minute. Decorate with flaked almonds.

triple chocolate
& vanilla mug cake

....

INGREDIENTS

1 slice of butter 1 cm (½ in) thick
   (30 g/1 oz)
1 egg
2 tablespoons light brown sugar
1½ teaspoons vanilla sugar or
   ½ teaspoon vanilla extract
1 tablespoon single (light) cream
5 tablespoons plain (all-purpose) flour
½ teaspoon baking powder
2 tablespoons dark, milk and
  white chocolate chips (30–35 g/1–1¼ oz)
  or 3 squares of dark chocolate +
  3 squares of white chocolate
  + 3 squares of milk chocolate,
  chopped into chips

DECORATION

a few mixed chocolate chips

In a mug: melt the butter for 30 seconds (800 watts).

One by one, beat in the egg, sugar, vanilla sugar, cream, flour and baking powder. Add the chocolate chips without stirring too much. Cook in the microwave for 1 minute 40 seconds (800 watts).

Decorate with a few mixed chocolate chips. Allow to cool for 1 minute before eating.

milk chocolate mug cake
with dark chocolate chips

....

INGREDIENTS

1 slice of butter 1 cm (½ in) thick
  (30 g/1 oz)
6 squares of milk chocolate (30 g/1 oz)
1 egg
2 tablespoons caster (superfine) sugar
5 tablespoons plain (all-purpose) flour
½ teaspoon baking powder
2 tablespoons dark chocolate chips
  (30 g/1 oz)

DECORATION

1 teaspoon dark chocolate chips

In a mug: melt the butter with the chocolate in the microwave for 30–40 seconds (800 watts).

Beat the mixture until smooth, then allow it to cool slightly. One by one, whisk in the egg, sugar, flour and baking powder. Add the dark chocolate chips without mixing too much.

Cook in the microwave for 1 minute 20 seconds (800 watts), then decorate with the chocolate chips. Allow to cool for 1 minute. The chocolate chips will melt into the mug cake before you eat it.

20
two flavours

white chocolate-coconut
& condensed milk mug cake

....

INGREDIENTS

1 slice of butter 1 cm (½ in) thick
   (30 g/1 oz)
6 squares of white chocolate or white
   chocolate with coconut (30 g/1 oz)
1 egg
2 tablespoons sweetened
   condensed milk
5 tablespoons plain (all-purpose) flour
½ teaspoon baking powder
2 tablespoons desiccated coconut

DECORATION

½ tablespoon desiccated coconut

In a mug: melt the butter with the chocolate in the microwave for 40 seconds (800 watts).

Beat the mixture until smooth, then allow it to cool slightly. One by one, whisk in the egg, condensed milk, flour, baking powder and coconut. Cook in the microwave for 1 minute 30 seconds (800 watts).

Allow to cool for 1 minute then sprinkle with the desiccated coconut.

22
two flavours

praline chocolate
& hazelnut mug cake

....

INGREDIENTS
1 slice of butter ½ cm (¼ in) thick
   (15 g/½ oz)
6 squares of praline chocolate (30 g/1 oz)
1 egg
2 tablespoons brown sugar
2 tablespoons milk
5 tablespoons plain (all-purpose) flour
¼ teaspoon baking powder
2 tablespoons ground hazelnuts

MIDDLE & DECORATION
1 square of praline chocolate (5 g/¼ oz)
1 teaspoon praline
2 teaspoons chopped hazelnuts

In a mug: melt the butter with the praline chocolate in the microwave for 30–40 seconds (800 watts).

Beat the mixture until smooth, then allow it to cool slightly. One by one, whisk in the egg, brown sugar, milk, flour, baking powder and ground hazelnuts. Cook in the microwave for 1 minute (800 watts). Push the the praline chocolate into the middle of the mixture and cook for a further 30 seconds.

Sprinkle with praline and chopped hazelnuts. Allow to cool for 1 minute before eating.

Oreo®
& milk chocolate mug cake

....

INGREDIENTS
1 slice of butter 1 cm (½ in) thick
  (30 g/1 oz)
3 squares of milk chocolate (15 g/½ oz)
1 egg
2 tablespoons single (light) cream
1 teaspoon vanilla sugar or
  a few drops of vanilla extract
4 tablespoons plain (all-purpose) flour
½ teaspoon baking powder
3 broken Oreo® biscuits (cookies)

DECORATION
1 broken Oreo® biscuit (cookie)

In a mug: melt the butter with the chocolate in the microwave for 30–40 seconds (800 watts).

Beat the mixture until smooth and allow it to cool slightly. One by one, whisk in the egg, cream, vanilla sugar, flour and baking powder. Add the broken Oreos® without stirring too much.

Cook in the microwave for 1 minute 30 seconds (800 watts). Decorate with the broken Oreo®.

Allow to cool for 1 minute before eating.

26
two flavours

Mont Blanc-style
choc-chestnut mug cake

....

INGREDIENTS

1 slice of butter 1 cm (½ in) thick
   (30 g/1 oz)
5 squares of dark or milk
   chocolate (25 g/1 oz)
1 egg
2 tablespoons light brown sugar
4 tablespoons plain (all-purpose) flour
½ teaspoon baking powder
1 tablespoon chestnut purée

DECORATION

1 teaspoon icing (confectioners') sugar,
   plus extra for sprinkling
2 tablespoons chestnut purée
1 tablespoon mascarpone cheese

In a mug: melt the butter with the chocolate in the microwave for 30–40 seconds (800 watts).

Beat the mixture until smooth, then allow it to cool slightly. One by one, whisk in the egg, sugar, flour, baking powder and chestnut purée. Cook in the microwave for 1 minute 30 seconds (800 watts).

In a seperate bowl, mix the icing sugar with the chestnut purée and mascarpone. Pour into a small piping bag fitted with a plain No. 2 writers nozzle and pipe out the purée in vermicelli-like strands. Sprinkle with icing sugar.

28
two flavours

banana & chocolate
mug cake with coconut

....

INGREDIENTS
1 slice of butter ½ cm (¼ in) thick
(15 g/½ oz)
6 squares of milk chocolate (30 g/1 oz)
½ mashed banana (50 g/2 oz)
1 egg
2 tablespoons light brown sugar
1 tablespoon desiccated coconut
4½ tablespoons plain (all-purpose) flour
½ teaspoon baking powder

DECORATION
a few slices of banana
a pinch of chocolate sprinkles
1 teaspoon desiccated coconut

In a mug: melt the butter with the chocolate in the microwave for 30–40 seconds (800 watts).

Beat the mixture until smooth, then allow it to cool slightly. One by one, whisk in the mashed banana, egg, sugar, coconut, flour and baking powder. Cook in the microwave for 1 minute 30 seconds (800 watts).

Place a few slices of banana on top, then decorate with chocolate sprinkles and desiccated coconut.

Allow to cool for 1 minute before eating.

30
two flavours

white chocolate & raspberry
mug cake with matcha green tea

INGREDIENTS

1 slice of butter 1 cm (½ in) thick
   (30 g/1 oz)
6 squares of white chocolate (30 g/1 oz)
1 egg
2 tablespoons caster (superfine) sugar
5 tablespoons plain (all-purpose) flour
½ teaspoon baking powder
½ teaspoon matcha green tea

MIDDLE & DECORATION

5 fresh raspberries

In a mug: melt the butter with the chocolate in the microwave for 30 seconds (800 watts).

Beat the mixture until smooth, then allow it to cool slightly. One by one, whisk in the egg, sugar, flour, baking powder and green tea.

Push 4 raspberries into the middle of the mixture. Cook in the microwave for 1 minute 40 seconds (800 watts).

Decorate with 1 raspberry. Allow to cool for 1 minute before eating.

32
two flavours

chocolate-orange
mug cake with cinnamon & icing

....

INGREDIENTS

1 slice of butter 1 cm (½ in) thick
   (30 g/1 oz)
6 squares of dark chocolate (30 g/1 oz)
1 egg
2 tablespoons light brown sugar
5 tablespoons plain (all-purpose) flour
½ teaspoon baking powder
1 tablespoon orange marmalade

ICING (FROSTING)

2 tablespoons icing (confectioners') sugar
2 drops of orange juice
1 teaspoon orange zest

DECORATION

1 teaspoon ground cinnamon
2 pieces of candied orange peel

In a mug: melt the butter with the chocolate in the microwave for 30–40 seconds (800 watts).

Beat the mixture until smooth, then allow it to cool slightly. One by one, whisk in the egg, sugar, flour and baking powder. Add the marmalade without stirring. Cook in the microwave for 1 minute 30 seconds (800 watts).

Allow to cool for 1 minute.

Mix all the ingredients to make the icing. Wait for 5 minutes for the icing mixture to set, then ice the mug cake, sprinkle with cinnamon and decorate with candied orange peel.

34
two flavours

Ovaltine®
milk chocolate mug cake

....

INGREDIENTS

1 slice of butter 1 cm (½ in) thick
   (30 g/1 oz)
6 squares of milk chocolate (30 g/1 oz)
1 egg
2 tablespoons muscovado or light
   brown sugar
3 tablespoons Ovaltine® powder
3 tablespoons single (light) cream
1½ teaspoons vanilla sugar or
   ½ teaspoon vanilla extract
3 tablespoons plain (all-purpose) flour
½ teaspoon baking powder

DECORATION

½ teaspoon Ovaltine®

In a mug: melt the butter with the chocolate in the microwave for 30–40 seconds (800 watts).

Beat the mixture until smooth, then allow it to cool slightly. One by one, whisk in the egg, sugar, Ovaltine®, cream, vanilla sugar, flour and baking powder. Cook in the microwave for 1 minute 20 seconds (800 watts).

Allow to cool for 1 minute and sprinkle with Ovaltine®.

dark chocolate
black forest mug cake

....

INGREDIENTS

1 slice of butter 1 cm (½ in) thick
   (30 g/1 oz)
6 squares of dark chocolate (30 g/1 oz)
1 egg
2 tablespoons brown sugar
5 tablespoons plain (all-purpose) flour,
   plus extra for sprinkling
½ teaspoon baking powder
30 g/1 oz drained pitted cherries
   in syrup

DECORATION

whipped cream
1 tablespoon dark chocolate flakes

In a mug: melt the butter with the chocolate in the microwave for 30–40 seconds (800 watts).

Beat the mixture until smooth, then allow it to cool slightly. One by one, whisk in the egg, sugar, flour and baking powder. Sprinkle the cherries with a little flour and add them to the mug without stirring too much. Cook in the microwave for 1 minute 20 seconds (800 watts).

Allow to cool for 1 minute. Decorate with whipped cream and chocolate flakes. Eat immediately – the whipped cream melts very quickly!

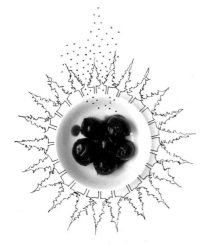

praline chocolate
& macadamia nut mug cake

....

INGREDIENTS
1 slice of butter 1 cm (½ in) thick
   (30 g/1 oz)
7 squares of praline chocolate
   (35 g/1¼ oz)
1 egg
2 tablespoons brown sugar
5 tablespoons plain (all-purpose) flour
½ teaspoon baking powder
5 macadamia nuts (20 g/¾ oz)

DECORATION
a few crushed macadamia or brazil nuts

In a mug: melt the butter with the chocolate in the microwave for 30–40 seconds (800 watts).

Beat the mixture until smooth, then allow it to cool slightly. One by one, whisk in the egg, sugar, flour and baking powder. Add the macadamia nuts without stirring too much. Cook in the microwave for 1 minute 20 seconds (800 watts).

Decorate with crushed nuts. Allow to cool for 1 minute before eating.

raspberry-choc
mug cake with chilli

....

INGREDIENTS

1 slice of unsalted or slightly salted
   butter 1 cm (½ in) thick (30 g/1 oz)
6 squares of dark chocolate (30 g/1 oz)
   at least 65 % cocoa
1 egg
2 tablespoons light brown sugar
4 tablespoons plain (all-purpose) flour
½ teaspoon baking powder
½ teaspoon chilli powder, or to taste
4–5 raspberries

DECORATION

¼ teaspoon chilli powder

In a mug: melt the butter with the chocolate in the microwave for 30–40 seconds (800 watts).

Beat the mixture until smooth, then allow it to cool slightly. One by one, whisk in the egg, sugar, flour and baking powder. Add the chilli powder and raspberries without stirring too much. Cook in the microwave for 1 minute 30 seconds (800 watts).

Sprinkle with chilli powder. Allow to cool for 1 minute before eating.

Nutella®
mug cake

....

INGREDIENTS
1 slice of butter 1 cm (½ in) thick
    (30 g/1 oz)
3 tablespoons Nutella®
1 egg
3 tablespoons light brown sugar
4 tablespoons plain (all-purpose) flour
½ teaspoon baking powder

MIDDLE
1 teaspoon Nutella®

In a mug: melt the butter with the Nutella® in the microwave for 30 seconds (800 watts).

Beat the mixture until smooth, then allow it to cool slightly. One by one, whisk in the egg, sugar, flour and baking powder. Cook in the microwave for 40 seconds (800 watts). Spoon the Nutella® into the middle and cook for a further 40 seconds.

Allow to cool for 1 minute before eating.

44
melt-in-the-middle

dark chocolate
mug cake with a peanut butter middle

....

INGREDIENTS

1 slice of butter 1 cm (½ in) thick
   (30 g/1 oz)
6 squares of dark chocolate (30 g/1 oz)
1½ teaspoons peanut butter
1 egg
1 tablespoon soft brown sugar
5 tablespoons plain (all-purpose) flour
½ teaspoon baking powder

MIDDLE & DECORATION

1 teaspoon peanut butter
1 teaspoon chocolate sprinkles

In a mug: melt the butter with the chocolate in the microwave for 30–40 seconds (800 watts).

Beat the mixture until smooth, then allow it to cool slightly. One by one, whisk in the peanut butter, egg, sugar, flour and baking powder. Cook in the microwave for 50 seconds (800 watts). Push the spoonful of peanut butter into the middle and cook for a further 40 seconds.

Decorate with chocolate sprinkles. Allow to cool for 1 minute before eating.

choc-coffee
mug cake with a soft caramel middle

....

INGREDIENTS

1 slice of slightly salted butter 1 cm
   (½ in) thick (30 g/1 oz)
8 squares of milk chocolate (40 g/1½ oz)
1 teaspoon coffee extract
1 egg
2 tablespoons light brown sugar
5 tablespoons plain (all-purpose) flour
½ teaspoon baking powder

MIDDLE

1 soft caramel

In a mug: melt the butter with the chocolate in the microwave for 30–40 seconds (800 watts).

Beat the mixture until smooth, add the coffee extract, then allow it to cool slightly. One by one, whisk in the egg, sugar, flour and baking powder. Cook in the microwave for 40 seconds (800 watts). Gently push the soft caramel into the middle and cook for a further 50 seconds.

Allow to cool for 1 minute before eating.

dark chocolate
mug cake with a caramelised biscuit middle

....

INGREDIENTS

1 slice of butter ½ cm (¼ in) thick
   (15 g/½ oz)
6 squares of dark chocolate (30 g/1 oz)
1 egg
1 teaspoon single (light) cream
2 tablespoons brown sugar
2 tablespoons crushed Lotus® or
   other caramelised biscuits (cookies)
5 tablespoons plain (all-purpose) flour
½ teaspoon baking powder

MIDDLE & DECORATION

1 teaspoon homemade caramelised
   biscuit spread (melted butter,
   caramelised biscuits (cookies) and
   condensed milk)
½ teaspoon crushed Lotus® or
   other caramelised biscuits (cookies)

In a mug: melt the butter with the chocolate in the microwave for 30–40 seconds (800 watts).

Beat the mixture until smooth, then allow it to cool slightly. One by one, whisk in the egg, cream, sugar, crushed biscuits, flour and baking powder. Cook in the microwave for 50 seconds (800 watts). Push the biscuit spread into the middle and cook for a further 40 seconds.

Allow to cool for 1 minute. Sprinkle with the crushed biscuit before eating.

50
melt-in-the-middle

tonka bean & vanilla
mug cake with a dark chocolate middle

....

INGREDIENTS
1 slice of butter 1 cm (½ in) thick
　(30 g/1 oz)
1 egg
1 tablespoon granulated sugar
1 tablespoon vanilla sugar or
　1 teaspoon vanilla extract
5 tablespoons plain (all-purpose) flour
½ teaspoon baking powder
½ teaspoon grated tonka bean or
　½ vanilla pod, seeds scraped

MIDDLE
1 large square of dark chocolate

In a mug: melt the butter in the microwave for 30 seconds (800 watts).

One by one, whisk in the egg, sugar, vanilla sugar, flour, baking powder and grated tonka bean. Cook in the microwave for 40 seconds (800 watts). Push the square of dark chocolate into the middle and cook for a further 50 seconds.

Allow to cool for 1 minute before eating.

milk chocolate
mug cake with a salted caramel middle

....

INGREDIENTS
1 slice of slightly salted butter
   1 cm (½ in) thick (30 g/1 oz)
5 squares of milk chocolate (25 g/1 oz)
1 egg
2 tablespoons caster (superfine) sugar
4 tablespoons plain (all-purpose) flour
½ teaspoon baking powder

MIDDLE & DECORATION
1 large teaspoon salted caramel sauce
a pinch of chocolate sprinkles

In a mug: melt the butter with the chocolate in the microwave for 30–40 seconds (800 watts).

Beat the mixture until smooth, then allow it to cool slightly. One by one, whisk in the egg, sugar, flour and baking powder. Cook in the microwave for 50 seconds (800 watts). Put the caramel sauce into the middle and cook for a further 40 seconds.

Allow to cool for 1 minute. Decorate with chocolate sprinkles before eating.

milk chocolate & hazelnut
melt-in-the-middle mug cake

....

INGREDIENTS
1 slice of butter 1 cm (½ in)
  thick (30 g/1 oz)
7 squares of milk chocolate (35 g/1¼ oz)
1 egg
2 tablespoons caster (superfine) sugar
3 tablespoons plain (all-purpose) flour
2 tablespoons ground or
  chopped hazelnuts
½ teaspoon baking powder

MIDDLE & DECORATION
1 square of hazelnut chocolate (5 g/¼ oz)
a few crushed hazelnuts

In a mug: melt the butter with the chocolate in the microwave for 30–40 seconds (800 watts).

Beat the mixture until smooth, then allow it to cool slightly. One by one, whisk in the egg, sugar, flour, ground hazelnuts and baking powder. Cook in the microwave for 50 seconds (800 watts). Push the hazelnut chocolate square into the middle and cook for a further 40 seconds.

Allow to cool for 1 minute. Sprinkle with the crushed hazelnuts before eating.

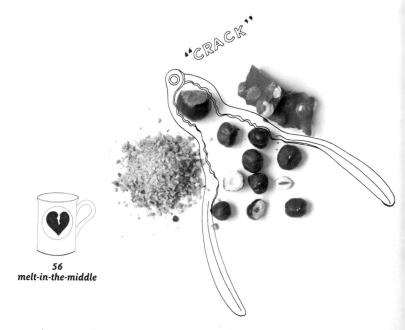

"CRACK"

dulce de leche
melt-in-the-middle mug cake

....

INGREDIENTS

1 slice of butter 1 cm (½ in) thick
　(30 g/1 oz)
6 squares of milk or dark chocolate
　(30 g/1 oz)
1 egg
2 tablespoons light brown sugar
5 tablespoons plain (all-purpose) flour
½ teaspoon baking powder
2 wafer curls (rolled wafers), crumbled

MIDDLE & DECORATION

2 tablespoons *dulce de leche*
　(caramelised milk)
½ teaspoon curls (rolled wafers),
　crumbled

In a mug: melt the butter with the chocolate in the microwave for 30–40 seconds (800 watts).

Beat the mixture until smooth, then allow it to cool slightly. One by one, whisk in the egg, sugar, flour and baking powder. Sprinkle some crumbled wafer curls on top and reserve a little for decorating. Cook in the microwave for 50 seconds (800 watts). Add the *dulce de leche* to the middle and cook for a further 40 seconds.

Allow to cool for 1 minute. Sprinkle the remaining wafer curls on top before eating.

white chocolate
mug cake with a raspberry middle

....

INGREDIENTS

1 slice of butter 1 cm (½ in) thick
   (30 g/1 oz)
8 squares of white chocolate
   (40 g/1½ oz)
1 egg
2 tablespoons caster (superfine) sugar
5 tablespoons plain (all-purpose) flour
½ teaspoon baking powder

MIDDLE & DECORATION

1 tablespoon raspberry jam (jelly)
½ teaspoon icing (confectioners') sugar

In a mug: melt the butter with the chocolate in the microwave for 30–40 seconds (800 watts).

Beat the mixture until smooth, then allow it to cool slightly. One by one, whisk in the egg, sugar, flour and baking powder. Cook in the microwave for 40 seconds (800 watts). Add the jam to the middle and cook for a further 50 seconds.

Allow to cool for 1 minute and lightly sprinkle with the icing sugar.

pistachio
mug cake with a white chocolate middle

....

INGREDIENTS

1 slice of butter ½ cm (¼ in) thick
   (15 g/½ oz)
5 squares of white chocolate (25 g/1 oz)
1 egg
1 tablespoon caster (superfine) sugar
½ teaspoon pistachio paste
5 tablespoons plain (all-purpose) flour
½ teaspoon baking powder

MIDDLE & DECORATION

1 square of white chocolate (5 g/¼ oz)
1 teaspoon melted white chocolate
a few crushed pistachios

In a mug: melt the butter with the chocolate in the microwave for 30–40 seconds (800 watts).

Beat the mixture until smooth, then allow the mug to cool slightly. One by one, whisk in the egg, sugar, pistachio paste, flour and baking powder. Cook in the microwave for 50 seconds (800 watts). Push the square of white chocolate into the middle and cook for a further 40 seconds.

Allow to cool for 1 minute. Dollop the melted white chocolate on top and sprinkling with the crushed pistachios before eating.

cappuccino
mug cake with whipped cream

....

INGREDIENTS

1 slice of butter 1 cm (½ in) thick
  (30 g/1 oz)
6 squares of dark chocolate (30 g/1 oz)
1 egg
2 tablespoons caster (superfine) sugar
5 tablespoons plain (all-purpose) flour
½ teaspoon baking powder
1 tablespoon instant coffee
1 tablespoon single (light) cream
1 drop of coffee extract

DECORATION

whipped cream
1 teaspoon unsweetened cocoa powder

In a mug: melt the butter with the chocolate in the microwave for 30–40 seconds (800 watts).

Beat the mixture until smooth, then allow it to cool slightly. One by one, whisk in the egg, sugar, flour, baking powder, instant coffee and cream. Add the drop of coffee extract and draw a spiral with the tip of a knife. Cook in the microwave for 1 minute 30 seconds (800 watts).

Allow to cool for 1 minute. Decorate with whipped cream and cocoa powder. Eat straight away – the whipped cream melts quickly!

64
swirls

chocolate-vanilla
marble mug cake

....

INGREDIENTS

5 squares of dark chocolate (25 g/1 oz)
1 slice of butter 1 cm (½ in) thick
   (30 g/1 oz)
1 egg
1 tablespoon vanilla sugar or
   1 teaspoon vanilla extract
1 tablespoon single (light) cream
2 tablespoons caster (superfine) sugar
5 tablespoons plain (all-purpose) flour
½ teaspoon baking powder

DECORATION

a pinch of sprinkles
½ teaspoon icing (confectioners') sugar

In a bowl: melt the chocolate in the microwave for 50 seconds (800 watts).

In a second bowl: melt the butter for 30–40 seconds (800 watts) and allow it to cool slightly. One by one, whisk in the egg, vanilla sugar, cream, sugar, flour and baking powder. Incorporate half of this mixture into the melted chocolate and beat together.

Pour the plain mixture and the chocolatey mixture alternately into a mug. Cook for 1 minute 40 seconds (800 watts).

Allow to cool for 1 minute. Dust with icing sugar and top with sprinkles before eating.

66
swirls

marshmallow swirl

milk chocolate mug cake

....

INGREDIENTS

1 slice of butter 1 cm (½ in) thick
(30 g/1 oz)
6 squares of milk chocolate (30 g/1 oz)
1 egg
2 tablespoons caster (superfine) sugar
5 tablespoons plain (all-purpose) flour
½ teaspoon baking powder
1 tablespoon Marshmallow Fluff®
or 3 melted marshmallows

In a mug: melt the butter with the chocolate in the microwave for 30–40 seconds (800 watts).

Beat the mixture until smooth, then allow it to cool slightly. One by one, whisk in the egg, sugar, flour and baking powder. Cook in the microwave for 30 seconds (800 watts). Add the Marshmallow Fluff® or melted marshmallows to the middle, swirl once with the spoon and cook for a further 60 seconds.

Allow to cool for 1 minute before eating. The marshmallow should ooze out of the mug.

fluff

dream

68
swirls

dark chocolate

& cream cheese swirl mug cake

....

INGREDIENTS

30 g (1 oz) Philadelphia® cream cheese
1 tablespoon milk
1 slice of slightly salted butter
   1 cm (½ in) thick (30 g/1 oz)
6 squares of dark chocolate (30 g/1 oz)
1 egg
2 tablespoons caster (superfine) sugar
4 tablespoons plain (all-purpose) flour
½ teaspoon baking powder

In a bowl: mix the cream cheese and milk together with a mini whisk.

In a mug: melt the butter with the chocolate in the microwave for 30–40 seconds (800 watts).

Beat the chocolate mixture until smooth, then allow it to cool slightly. One by one, whisk in the egg, sugar, flour and baking powder. Add the cream cheese without mixing too much. Cook in the microwave for 1 minute 30 seconds (800 watts).

Allow to cool for 1 minute before eating.

**70
swirls**

Our thanks

To Pauline, Aurélie and Géraldine, for their support,
reading the manuscript and suggestions for the graphics.

To Olivier for his helping hand almost daily.

Shopping for mugs

BHV, www.bhv.fr

Mug Cakes Chocolate by Sandra Mahut
© Hachette Livre Books (Marabout)
This English launguage edition published in 2015 by Hardie Grant Books

Hardie Grant Books (UK)
5th & 6th Floors
52-54 Southwark Street
London SE1 1UN
www.hardiegrant.co.uk

Hardie Grant Books (Australia)
Ground Floor, Building 1
658 Church Street
Melbourne, VIC 3121
www.hardiegrant.com.au

The moral rights of Sandra Mahut to be identified as the author
of this work have been asserted by her in accordance with the
Copyright, Designs and Patents Act 1988.

Text © Sandra Mahut 2014

All rights reserved. No part of this publication may be reproduced,
stored in a retrieval system or transmitted in any form by any
means, electronic, electrostatic, magnetic tape, mechanical,
photocopying, recording or otherwise, without the prior written
permission of the Publisher.

British Library Cataloguing-in-Publication Data. A catalogue record
for this book is available from the British Library.

ISBN: 978-1-78488009-5

Illustrations: Jane Teasdale
Page Design: Frédéric Voisin
Translator: Gilla Evans
Typesetter: David Meikle
Printed and bound in Spain by Graficas Estella
Find this book on Cooked.
Cooked.com.au
Cooked.com
10 9 8 7 6 5